W9-ASO-686

EX LIBRIS

MARY E. R. ZIMMERMAN

CAVES TO CATHEDRALS

A Greek Orthodox church in the town of Mystras, Greece, which became a religious center after the fall of Constantinople in 1492. Typical of most small churches in the Balkan countries, it is of stone and brick, with red tile roofs.

CAVES TO CATHEDRALS

Architecture of the World's Great Religions

by
Carl E. Hiller

Little, Brown and Company
BOSTON · TORONTO

J
726
H
Rare
Book
Room

COPYRIGHT © 1974 BY CARL E. HILLER

ALL RIGHTS RESERVED. NO PART OF THIS BOOK MAY BE REPRODUCED
IN ANY FORM OR BY ANY ELECTRONIC OR MECHANICAL MEANS IN-
CLUDING INFORMATION STORAGE AND RETRIEVAL SYSTEMS WITHOUT
PERMISSION IN WRITING FROM THE PUBLISHER, EXCEPT BY A REVIEWER
WHO MAY QUOTE FROM BRIEF PASSAGES IN A REVIEW.

FIRST EDITION

T 11/74

Library of Congress Cataloging in Publication Data

Hiller, Carl E.
    Caves to cathedrals.

    Bibliography: p. 133
    1. Churches—Juvenile literature.   2. Synagogues—
Juvenile literature.   3. Temples—Juvenile literature.
4. Mosques—Juvenile literature.   [1. Churches.
2. Synagogues.   3. Temples.   4. Mosques.   5. Reli-
gions]   I. Title.
NA4600.H54   726   74-16188

ISBN 0-316-36395-2

Published simultaneously in Canada
by Little, Brown & Company (Canada) Limited

PRINTED IN THE UNITED STATES OF AMERICA

Contents

Acknowledgments

FOR THEIR ADVICE and help the author wishes to thank Mr. Abdisalam Adam, Mr. Tadesse Araya, Ms. Ruth A. Bookbinder, Father Charles Cushing, Dr. Lucjan Dobroszycki, Mr. Frank Graham, Dr. Howard Hamilton, Mr. William Hennelly, Miss Anna Kleeband, Rabbi Saul Kraft, Mrs. Rose Lehrer, Ms. Lois Lord, Mr. Anand Mohan, Mrs. Nettie Osofsky, Mr. Brian Percival, Professor Erich Rosenthal, Mr. David B. Sommer, Miss Chin-Pin Wu, and Professor Pei-Yi Wu. The author is also indebted to the editorial staff of *Life* for ideas and facts in *The World's Great Religions*, published by Time, Inc.

CAVES TO CATHEDRALS

Introduction

FOR THOUSANDS OF YEARS men have sought to explain the mystery of life. In their search for the meaning of life itself, of birth, death, the change of seasons, the sun, rain, day, night, floods and drought, people in different parts of the world have developed a variety of beliefs, some simple, some complex. Most of these beliefs revolve around the superhuman power of a god — or gods. A system of beliefs, with accompanying practices and rituals that have evolved around them, is usually called a religion.

A number of the world's religions have grown, flourished, and then disappeared. The religion of the ancient Greeks, adopted by the Romans, was gradually replaced by the growing Christian religion. The religions of the Aztecs, the Incas, and the Mayas of the Western Hemisphere disappeared when those great civilizations came to an end with the arrival of the conquering Spanish.

Although there are many religions in the world today the most influential ones, and those with the most numerous devotees, are probably Hinduism, Buddhism, Judaism, Christianity and Islam, each with its various divisions and offshoots.

The followers of each religion have created structures to serve as the places of worship of the god or gods of that religion. Some of these structures are buildings or shrines in which only a selected group of people — such as priests — may enter. Others are buildings where all followers of the religion may gather to worship. Most structures created for religious purposes have been influenced by the prevailing styles of the region or of the historical period in which they were built. Simple or elaborate, these structures include some of the most beautiful architectural creations of man.

Hinduism

PERHAPS the oldest of all the world's living religions, Hinduism evolved in the region that is now India and Pakistan. It is today the religion of more than 300,000,000 people in India and about 15,000,000 in other parts of the world. The word *Hindu* is thought to have been derived from the word *Indus*, a river in the valley of which an earlier civilization existed. This Indus Valley civilization was overrun about 1700 B.C. by a people from the west known as Aryans, who brought with them their own religion.

Over the years that religion evolved into Hinduism, which is a total way of life as well as a set of beliefs. To the Hindus all life is sacred and God is everywhere. God is a universal spirit known as Brahman. At the same time, however, Hindus believe in a myriad of other gods, all aspects of the one divine spirit. Chief of the deities in the pantheon are Brahma, Vishnu and Shiva — the Hindu trinity.

Brahma is the Creator of all. Vishnu is the Preserver and Shiva is the Destroyer. Vishnu, the Preserver, keeps the world going, and is usually thought of as the god of love. He, according to tradition, has come to earth as a human many times. Two favorites among his incarnations are Rama, thought of as the ideal man, and Krishna, a hero. Shiva, the Destroyer, rids the world of the old in order to make room for the new. These gods are worshipped in many forms and even with different names.

The goal of the Hindu is to rise above the material world and to achieve a oneness with God. To attain such a goal the devout Hindu not only participates in prayer and ritual, but behaves in his daily life according to certain precepts that include truth, nonviolence, charity, and compassion toward all living creatures.

Each god has a specific member of the animal kingdom as his or her mount. Since Shiva, one of the trinity, and thus one of the most important of the gods, has a bull as his mount, bulls are especially venerated.

Rebirth is part of the Hindu belief. One will be reborn in a future life in accordance with one's behavior in this life. The record of one's behavior through his various lives is called Karma.

As do all religions, Hinduism has undergone constant change. Today there is less emphasis on image worship than in the past, and more attention is given to an exaltation of spiritual ideas.

The scriptures of the Hindu religion consist of three groups: the Vedas, the Brahmanas, and the Upanishads. The Vedas are the oldest prayers, the Brahmanas are concerned with the ritual of worship, and the Upanishads are logical arguments to questions about God, man and the universe — the real philosophical basis of the Hindu religion.

The Shore Temple at Mamallapuram, India, built in the eighth century. The smaller of the two parts of the temple is the mandapa, a columned porch.

Hindu Temples

ALMOST EVERY VILLAGE in India has its temple; some have more than one. The temple's architecture was intended to differ from that of the homes of the people not only to reflect its purpose as a spiritual center, but also to dominate its surroundings. Most Hindu temples are so almost completely covered with richly carved sculptural ornament that their architectural features are actually subordinated to the carver's skill. Although there is some abstract carved ornament on the interior and exterior surfaces of the temples, most of the sculpture is of figures of gods, goddesses, processions, battle scenes, elephants and horses. Sometimes entire legends are depicted in the carvings.

Hindu temples are built to enshrine the images of gods, goddesses or saints, and each temple is dedicated to one of the many Hindu gods.

There are several principal parts of every Hindu temple. A small, square, dark cell, the garbha-griha, houses the image of the gods, which is usually carved in stone. Over this cell rises a tower called a sikhara or vimana. A large hall, usually lined with pillars, where the devotees gather to worship is the mandapa. Connecting the garbha-griha and the mandapa is a rectangular chamber or vestibule, the antarala.

In southern India temples are generally more extensive, usually including a courtyard or loggia, a pool, and sometimes a series of smaller temples grouped around the main sanctuary. A wall may enclose the entire complex.

The temple in India is far more than a place of worship; it is the center of most of the educational, cultural, and recreational life of the community. Hindu worship is an individual or family affair. A person — or a family group — enters the temple bringing fruit and flowers as offerings to the god or goddess of the temple. A priest accepts the offerings that have been placed on or before the god's image, and then returns them to the worshippers. They, in turn, then prostrate themselves before the image. The local assembly meets in the temple to discuss and settle municipal affairs. Intellectual discussions take place within its walls, and schools for the young are often attached to it. Religious ceremonies at the temple often include music and dancing.

Part of the Kailasanath Temple at Ellora, India. One of the famous rock-cut temples, it was carved out of a hillside in the eighth century B.C.

View of Mandapa of Cave Temple at Elephanta, an island off the Indian coast near Bombay. Many of the early Hindu temples such as this one were carved out of living rock. Dating from the eighth century B.C.E., this temple was dedicated to the god Shiva.

Muktesvara Temple, Bhuvaneshwar, Orissa, India, ninth–tenth centuries. The form of this temple and others similar to it in eastern India came from earlier structures made of tall reeds which were bent inward toward their top, with their heads tied together in a bunch.

The Temple of Surya (the Sun) at Konarak in north-
eastern India, sometimes called the Black Pagoda. Built
in the thirteenth century, it was designed to resemble a
huge chariot drawn by the seven horses of the sun.
Note the huge carved wheels along the base wall.

One of the twelve wheels of the Temple of Surya at
Konarak. Each of them is ten feet in diameter, and is
covered with intricate carving.

A detail of some of the thousands of sculptured figures that adorn the exterior of the eleventh-century temples at Khajuraho in central India.

Kesava Temple, Somnathpur, India, thirteenth century. Characteristic of this and other temples of Mysore in southern India is the star-shaped ground plan and raised platform on which it stands. Extremely rich decoration covers its surface.

Detail of the elaborate ornamental sculpture on the Kesava Temple at Somnathpur.

The Great Temple at Madura in southern India, seventeenth century. Two of its eleven tower gateways (gopura) soar above a cloister and a pool used for ritual ablutions. The temple is a huge complex of many buildings, in the center of which is an immense courtyard designed to hold crowds who gather to watch religious processions.

One of the imposing gopura of the Great Temple at Madura. Its entire surface is carved with sculptures of Hindu deities.

Pillared corridor (Alindka) of the Rameswaram Temple, India, built in the seventeenth century. Four thousand feet long, the spacious hall is lined with intricately carved columns.

Lord Shiva's bull, Nandi, at Chamundi, Mysore. This magnificent sculpture of the sacred animal is about three times the height of an adult.

The banks of the Ganges River in the holy city of
Benares. Devout Hindus pray and rest on its banks and
bathe in its sacred waters to wash away all sins.

16

Buddhism

THE RELIGION of several million people chiefly of eastern Asian countries, Buddhism developed from the teachings of a man who grew up in India in the sixth century B.C. The son of an Indian chief or prince, Siddhartha Gautama was raised in the Hindu religion. Living amidst the luxuries of a wealthy family, he was protected by his father from any knowledge or awareness of the world outside the family circle. At the age of twenty-nine his eyes were opened to the fact that there were people less fortunate than he, that old age, poverty, disease and human misery were rampant in the world.

Rejecting the pleasures and comforts he had known, he left home and wandered for six years in search of answers to the questions that were troubling him about human suffering. After much self-imposed physical hardship and soul-searching he finally felt that he had discovered the riddle of life and was enlightened. Siddhartha was known thereafter by the name Buddha — the Enlightened One.

Buddha had never planned to found a formal religion any more than had Jesus. But his teachings attracted many followers or disciples. He founded an order of brothers — or monks — setting down the precepts by which they should live.

Buddha believed that man's destiny was not in the hands of the gods, but that man was master of his own destiny and that his salvation was dependent on his own actions. Those actions were codified into a pattern of self-discipline not unlike the Ten Commandments of Judaism and Christianity. Described as the Five Precepts, they precluded the taking of life (killing), taking what is not given (stealing), illicit pleasures, lying, and drinking intoxicating beverages.

The basis of Buddhism lies in Buddha's concept of the Four Noble Truths and the Eightfold Path to man's salvation. The Truths, as he conceived them, are:

• That all life is a series of sorrows and suffering.

• That all suffering stems from a craving or desire for the pleasures of life.

• That an end to suffering can only be achieved by an end to the craving for pleasures.

• That an end to the craving lies in following an Eightfold Path.

The steps, then, in the Eightfold Path are Right Belief, Right Aims, Right Speech, Right Actions, Right Occupations, Right Endeavor, Right Thinking, and Right Meditation. By following these precepts in a path somewhere between asceticism and a worldly life — the middle path — through many successive lives one will finally achieve a state of bliss or infinity called Nirvana.

Buddha's teachings were carried on after his death by his disciples. Eventually differences as to the interpretation of those teachings developed, and as a result two distinct forms of Buddhism evolved: Hinayana and Mahayana. Missionary monks carried Hinayana to such countries as Cambodia, Laos, Burma, Ceylon and Siam (now Thailand). Mahayana, known as northern Buddhism, spread to China, Tibet, Mongolia, Korea and Japan.

Although Buddhists did not at first create images of the Master, they used symbols as an aid in remembering him. One such symbol was the wheel — the symbol of the Law, or Eternal Truth. The law is set in motion by the turning of the wheel. The umbrella symbolizes the spiritual king. The lotus symbolizes the purity of the human spirit. Floating on the surface of the water with its roots anchored in the mud below, it is not sullied by the mud. In the same way, the human spirit may remain pure whatever the environment. Paintings and sculptures of Buddha usually show him seated or standing on a lotus blossom.

Eventually, as Buddhism spread throughout Asia, images of Buddha himself were created and became objects of reverence.

Buddhist Temples and Shrines

THE EARLIEST STRUCTURES that served as Buddhist shrines were great circular mounds of stone. In India these monuments, erected to guard the relics of Buddha, are called stupas; elsewhere in Asia they are called pagodas or dagobas.

As is the case of places of worship of most of the world's religions, there is no one architectural form or style that can be recognized as uniquely Buddhist. Styles of Buddhist temples usually differ from country to country. The temples of Burma have a distinct form of their own, as do those of Thailand, Cambodia, Ceylon, China and Japan.

Whatever their shape or style they usually are highly ornate, both inside and out. Much use of gold leaf is made on the temples of Burma. Elaborate carving, covered with brilliant colors — usually blue, red and green — is typical of Chinese Buddhist temples. The exterior walls of Thailand's temples are of tile or bits of mirrors, precious stones and glass set into plaster or gilded wood. Late Buddhist temples in Japan, however, are typically very simple and austere, constructed of unfinished wood.

The Buddhist form of worship, much like that of the Hindu, is an individual or family affair. Flower and fruit offerings are placed on or before the image of Buddha. The offerings are accepted by a priest. In Hinayana Buddhism, the worshipper spends more time in front of the image of Buddha in silent meditation.

The images of Buddha, usually housed in the temples, but sometimes placed in outdoor settings, are of stone, bronze, or wood painted or covered with gold leaf. Some of them show Buddha seated in a meditative pose; others portray him in a reclining position to symbolize his having reached the ultimate state of repose, or Nirvana.

The Dhamek Stupa at Sarnath near Banaras, India, third century B.C. It commemorates the first sermon preached by Buddha and is probably the earliest surviving religious structure in India. Flags and pennants are displayed for celebrations of Buddha's birthday and the day of his enlightenment.

Stupa at Sanchi, second century B.C. The dome symbolized the universe; the four gates, the winds. The largest and best preserved of the stupas in India. Crowning the dome is a many-tiered and gilded umbrella, a form of pagoda.

Detail of the north gateway (torana) of the stupa at Sanchi. The elaborate carving illustrates legends about Buddha.

The Bodh Gaya Temple at Bihar in eastern India. Built at the spot where Buddha attained enlightenment, the imposing square pyramidal tower is 180 feet tall. At each corner is a small replica of the central tower. Each Buddhist priest has his own flag, usually yellow or saffron color, which is displayed on the temple at which he officiates.

Phra Pathom Chedi, dating from the year 150, is one of the oldest and largest temples of its kind in Thailand. In the Burmese style, it is in Nakhon Pathom, near Bangkok, where Buddhism was first introduced into Thailand.

Horyuji Temple, Nara, Japan. One of the great Buddhist shrines of Japan, the temple comprises about forty buildings. The five-story pagoda in the center of the picture was built in 607 and still contains the original timber used in its construction.

Todaiji Temple, Nara. Built in the eighth century, when Nara was Japan's capital. The largest wooden building in the world, the Daibutsuden, the main building of the temple, houses a huge seated image of Buddha.

The great bronze statue of Buddha in the Daibutsuden in Nara represents him in the act of preaching a sermon.

Borobudur Temple, Java. This huge five-storied pyramid was built in the ninth century. A central stupa is surrounded by three concentric circles of smaller stupas and flights of steps. Beautiful relief sculpture covers most of the surface areas.

*The Shwe Dagon Pagoda in Rangoon, Burma, one of
Buddhism's largest shrines.* The bell-shaped structure,
covered with gold leaf, is surrounded by a myriad of
smaller shrines and sculptured figures.

Angkor Wat, Cambodia, built in the twelfth century.
This huge complex of buildings, columned porticos and
terraces is set in the jungle and surrounded by walls
and a moat, and is nearly two and a half miles in cir-
cumference.

*Stairs leading to the main shrine of Angkor Wat, a
pyramidlike tower that dominates the whole temple.*

Lung Shan Temple in Taipei, the capital of Taiwan. A Buddhist temple originally built in 1738 and restored several times, it is dedicated to the Goddess of Mercy.

Detail of the roof ornamentation of the Lung Shan Temple. The elaborate carving is painted in brilliant red, blue and gold.

Wat Arun (*Temple of the Dawn*), *Thailand.* Towering 250 feet above the Chao Phraya River in Bangkok's twin city of Thon Buri, it was constructed of brick covered with stucco.

Wat Po (the Monastery of the Reclining Buddha). Part of a large temple complex in Bangkok, Thailand, it contains an image of a reclining Buddha 160 feet long.

Wat Phra Keo (the Chapel of the Emerald Buddha) in Bangkok. The personal chapel of the King of Thailand, it was built in 1784 to house a small green jasper image of Buddha.

Interior of the Wat Phra Keo in Bangkok. The golden sculptures, repeated in long rows, are images of the *garuda,* the king of of the birds. The garuda, shown holding two snakes, is the royal emblem of King Rama II, who had the chapel built.

Shinto

SHINTO, the ancient and traditional religion of Japan, developed as nature worship. Gods, called Kami, were assigned to all natural objects and phenomena. There are literally hundreds of Kami and they exist not only in all animate beings such as the wolf, the serpent, the wild boar, the tiger and even the silkworm, but also in all inanimate forms of nature: the soil, trees, mountains, waterfalls, sun, moon and waves. Endowed also with divinity are such natural phenomena as clouds, wind, thunder, fire and earthquakes.

Japanese mythology also attributed divinity to the Emperor as a direct descendant of the most important of all the Kami, Amaterasu-o-mi-Kami, the Sun Goddess. National and even local heroes are also considered Kami.

Chinese culture, including written language, painting, architecture and legal and social codes, was introduced into Japan, and began affecting all aspects of Japanese life in the sixth and seventh centuries. With it came Mahayana Buddhism. Only then did the name Shinto, Chinese for "the way of the gods," come into being, in contrast to "the way of Buddha."

In the eighth century Shinto was gradually overshadowed by Buddhism, when the Buddhist priests claimed that Shinto Kami were actually incarnations of Buddhas and Bodhisattvas. During a period of about a thousand years the two religions were more or less merged into one religion called Ryobu Shinto, "The Twofold Way of the Gods."

Later there was a revival of the earlier form of Shinto which has existed — with minor changes — until the present and coexists with Buddhism in Japan. One major change came about with Japan's defeat in World War II, when the Emperor disclaimed his divinity.

The ancient records of Shinto are the Kojiki — The Records of Ancient Matters.

Shinto Shrines

A PLACE OF WORSHIP in the Shinto religion is not necessarily always a man-made structure. A natural spot such as a tree, a waterfall or a mountain can serve as a sacred place where the worshipper comes to pray. Thousands of actual buildings do exist as shrines, however. Large or small, Shinto shrines are always extremely simple in design and are constructed of wood, the most abundant material in heavily forested Japan.

A typical shrine, such as the one at Ise, dedicated to the Sun Goddess, consists of an inner sanctuary (shoden) surrounded by several smaller buildings used as treasure houses (honden). The buildings are rectangular with curved, gabled roofs made of bark. Enclosing the complex of buildings is an inner fence and an outer fence, both pierced by decorative, ceremonial entrance gateways called torii. Torii are simple but extremely dignified wooden structures consisting of two upright posts connected at the top by two horizontal crossbars.

Worshippers at a Shinto shrine enter the enclosure through the various torii but are forbidden to enter the shoden, admittance to which is permitted only to priests. No images or idols are to be found in Shinto shrines because the followers of the religion think of their gods as invisible spirits.

Shinto prayer is an individual affair. Worshippers approach a shrine through a torii, which is an act of purification, then wash mouth and hands in a basin of water. After ringing a bell, they clap their hands several times, and pray silently with bowed heads. On special occasions a priest will bless a group of worshippers.

The shrine of Ise. Dedicated to the sun goddess, the inner shrine at Ise is considered the holiest place in Japan. Set in the midst of a forest, Ise's various buildings are made of the wood of the white cypress, planed smooth and left unfinished. Originally built in the fifth century, they are torn down every twenty years and reconstructed on a nearby site to symbolize the death and rebirth of all things in nature.

Pilgrims entering the outer torii of the shrine of Ise.
The second torii in front of them is as close to the
shrine as they are allowed.

The torii of the Itsukushima Shrine, rising from the water off the island of Miyajima.

*Itsukushima Shrine on the sacred island of Miyajima,
Japan* (*thirteenth century*). Many of the buildings of
the shrine are built on posts over the water, giving them
a feeling of floating.

Another view of the Itsukushima Shrine, with the torii used when approaching the shrine from the water.

Toshogu Shrine, Nikko, 1636. One of the most beautiful shrines in Japan. Surrounded by majestic trees, most of the buildings are lacquered in vermilion. At the left is a granite torii, and at the right a five-story pagoda in red and gold.

Heian Shrine, Kyoto. Built in 1895 to commemorate the
eleven hundredth anniversary of the founding of Kyoto,
its columns and other woodwork are painted a brilliant
vermilion.

Fujiyama, a quiescent volcano, is the most revered of all natural sites in Japan and is the scene of pilgrimages of thousands of Japanese annually.

Judaism

JUDAISM is not only important as a religion in its own right, but also as the basis for both Christianity and Islam. Its birthplace was Asia Minor, the region just east of the Mediterranean Sea, the period approximately 2500 to 2000 B.C.

The area was populated at that time by nomadic tribes of Semitic people, each headed by a sheikh or chief — usually the head of a large family. Much like the Bedouins of today the groups roamed the region searching constantly for new grazing land for their flocks.

What religions existed in that part of the world were based on superstition and the worship of statues or idols. One of the nomadic tribes, the Hebrews, had as its head man the patriarch Abraham. It is he who is given credit for the idea that there is but one God — all-powerful and all-pervasive. That concept, called monotheism, became the basis for not only Judaism, but also for its offshoots, Christianity and Islam.

The concept of an invisible or abstract God was not easily understood or readily accepted by the simple, uneducated Hebrews. The religion existed only tenuously for several hundred years.

About 1300 B.C., another Hebrew, Moses, added strength to Judaism in giving it its basic tenets. At that time, the Hebrews were slaves in Egypt and Moses had resolved to liberate his people from bondage. Not only was he successful in doing so, but while wandering with them in the desert he received a revelation that has served ever since as the basis for the religious and moral code of Judaism: The Ten Commandments.

One of the strongest and most persistent beliefs of the Jewish people is that of the coming of a savior or leader, called a Messiah.

The scriptures of Judaism consist of the sayings and writings of many Hebrew sages, prophets and judges gathered into one book, the Old Testament. The first five books of the Old Testament are especially revered, and, copied by hand on parchment scrolls, are known as the Torah. Two of the basic tenets of Judaism included in the Torah were the love of God and the love of one's fellow man. They were later stressed by Jesus in his teachings.

In the sixth century, commentaries on the Torah, as well as oral laws, were compiled into a huge work of many volumes called the Talmud.

Although the most sacred building of Judaism, the Temple in Jerusalem, was destroyed and the Jews widely dispersed as a result of periodic conquests of Palestine, it was the faith of the Jews that held them together and preserved Judaism as a religion.

As do most religions, Judaism has its various divisions and sects. The three chief groups are Orthodox, Conservative, and Reform Jews. Orthodox Jews, greatest in number, have retained the ancient customs and rituals of their ancestors. Conservative and Reform Jews have modified some of the customs in keeping with modern life.

Synagogues

THE SYNAGOGUE, historically, is not only a place of worship for Jews but serves as a place of assembly and of the study of the law (the Torah and the Talmud). As a place where congregants met together and participated in prayer and study it differed from the Temple in Jerusalem, where ritual had been performed only by a hereditary priesthood and Levites. Even before the Diaspora, but to a much greater extent later when Jews settled in groups in different parts of the world, the synagogue became the focal center of Jewish community life. Included in many synagogues was a school for children and rooms for the lodging of travelers. The word *synagogue* comes from the Greek word meaning gathering place or assembly.

Jewish worship is generally congregational in form and is usually led by a rabbi or sometimes by a member of the congregation. In Orthodox synagogues worshippers read aloud from prayer books, but not necessarily in unison. In all Jewish services there is often congregational singing, and a cantor (singer) sometimes chants or sings some of the prayers. A reading from the Torah is a feature of all Orthodox and Conservative synagogues, and also of many Reform synagogues.

Since traditionally only men participated actively in the religious services, whether on the Sabbath or on special occasions such as the holy day of Yom Kippur (the Day of Atonement) and the various festivals, a separate section was reserved for women. Such a section usually took the form of a balcony or gallery, sometimes screened by latticework. Orthodox Jews still retain this practice.

Neither Jewish law nor tradition prescribes any specific type of structure as a place for public worship. Any humble home or building can serve as long as there are ten adult males (a minyan) present.

Wherever Jews have settled in groups they have usually built synagogues, sometimes small and simple in character, sometimes large and highly elaborate, depending on the size and wealth of the congregation. The architectural style of these buildings usually follows that of the local style of the period in much the same way as do houses of worship of other religions. One feature is shared by all synagogues, however, and that is the Ark. Usually placed prominently at the eastern end of the interior, the Ark is most often a cupboard or niche in which is kept the Scroll of the Law — the Torah.

Another feature of the synagogue is a platform for the reader of the Torah, who can be either the rabbi, who is the spiritual leader of the congregation, or a parishioner. In Orthodox synagogues the platform is centrally placed. In Eastern European countries it is called the bimah; in Germany, the almemor; and in Sephardic synagogues the tebah.

The Wailing Wall in Jerusalem. It was the western retaining wall of the Temple built by King Herod of Judaea in 20 B.C. on the site of King Solomon's original Temple. Jews traditionally come here to lament the Temple's destruction — hence the phrase *Wailing Wall* — and to pray.

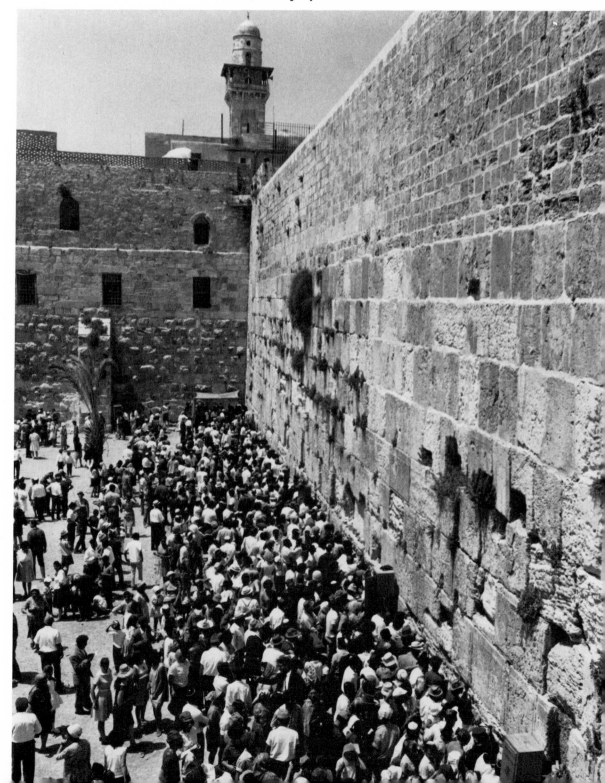

Rachel's Tomb, on the road between Jerusalem and Bethlehem. Since the patriarchs Abraham, Isaac and Jacob are revered by both Jews and Moslems, the tomb of Jacob's wife, Rachel, serves as a shrine for both religions. Here pious Jews pray for their sick.

Synagogue at Worms, built in the twelfth century when Worms was one of the three most important Jewish communities in Germany. It had been the oldest surviving synagogue in Germany until it was destroyed by the Nazis in 1938. The German government has since had it reconstructed, using old plans and some remaining stones.

The Altneuschul (literally Old New Synagogue) in Prague, built in the fourteenth century. Medieval in style, its narrow windows result in a dark, gloomy interior. It is probably the oldest synagogue in Europe still in use. The building at the right with the clock tower is the eighteenth-century Jewish Town Hall.

El Tránsito Synagogue, Toledo, Spain. Built in the fourteenth century in the Moorish style, which had been introduced into Spain when it was overrun by the Arabs of North Africa. After the expulsion of the Jews from Spain it became a church. The Ark stood at the far wall under the two windows, which in shape and position suggest the Tablets of the Law. The partially screened recesses at the upper right indicate the women's gallery.

Interior detail of El Tránsito Synagogue. The Hebrew inscriptions are verses from the Psalms (*Old Testament*). Alabaster panes in the windows admit a soft, diffused light.

Fortress synagogue at Luck, Poland, 1626–1628. King Sigismund III, in giving permission to the Jews of Luck to built a synagogue, imposed the condition that it should also serve as a fortress with cannon mounted on the roof, to help in the defense of the city against enemy attack. Luck (now spelled Lutsk), along with much of eastern Poland, was ceded to the U.S.S.R. after World War II, and the building now serves as a movie theater.

Synagogue at Suchowola, Poland, 1750. Wooden synagogues were very common in Poland, Lithuania and the Ukraine, where wood was the most plentiful building material. The triple-hipped roof saddled by a gabled one gave an impressive appearance to an otherwise simple square structure. Suchowola is also now in the Soviet Union.

The Portuguese Synagogue in Amsterdam, Holland.
Built in 1675 by descendants of the Jews who had been
expelled from Spain and Portugal during the Inquisi-
tion, many of whom settled in Holland. It is in the
baroque architectural style of the period, with pilasters,
arched windows and a balustrade above the cornice.

*Interior view of the Portuguese Synagogue in Amster-
dam.* At the left is the magnificent Ark crowned with
the Tablets of the Law (the Ten Commandments). At
the right is the tebah, and in the right background, the
women's gallery.

Mikvé Israel (Hope of Israel) Synagogue in Willemstad, Curaçao. Built in 1732, it is the earliest known synagogue in existence in the Western Hemisphere. Its chief architectural inspiration was the Portuguese Synagogue in Amsterdam, the city from whence came most of the first Jews to settle in the New World.

Interior of the Mikvé Israel Synagogue showing the tebah at the left, and the women's gallery at the upper right.

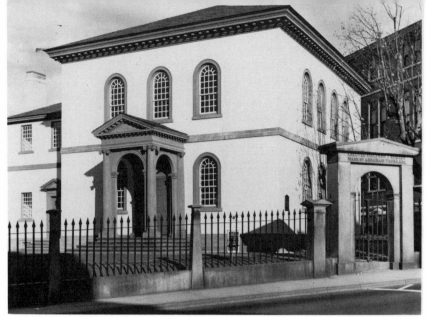

Congregation Jeshuat Israel, Newport, Rhode Island, 1763. Called the Touro Synagogue after its first minister, Rabbi Isaac Touro, it is the oldest surviving synagogue in the United States. Designed by Peter Harrison in the English Georgian style popular at the time in the Colonies, it is now a National Historic Site.

Interior of the Touro Synagogue, richly ornamented in contrast to the plain exterior. The lower balustrade surrounds the tebah; the upper one runs around the gallery reserved for women, which was typical of Sephardic congregations.

The Károly Körut Temple in Budapest, Hungary. **Built in 1859, a time when European and American architecture was undergoing a series of historical revivals, it combines Moorish and Byzantine styles in its use of towers, cupolas, colored marble and ornament.**

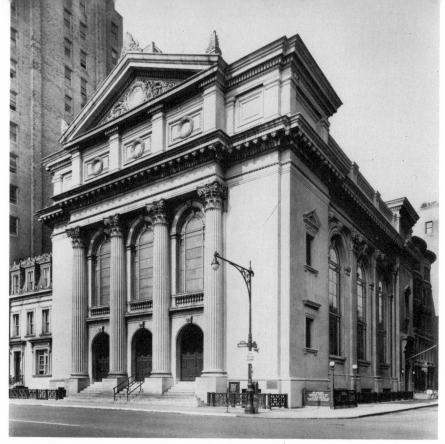

Temple Shearith Israel in New York, built in 1897. The fifth home of the oldest congregation in New York, it was designed by Arnold Brunner using classical forms related to Greco-Roman synagogue remains in Palestine.

Interior of Temple Shearith Israel, showing the traditional Sephardic synagogue plan. The tebah at the left is actually centered on the main floor, while the Ark, framed by paired columns, is at the right.

Park Synagogue and Community Center, Cleveland, Ohio, 1946–1952. Designed by Erich Mendelsohn, who was one of the foremost innovators of modern synagogue architecture, first in his native Germany and then in the United States. The large dome that covers the synagogue proper was a bold novel concept of Mendelsohn's.

Beth Shalom Congregation, Elkins Park, Pennsylvania, 1959. Designed by the great American architect Frank Lloyd Wright, it is built of corrugated plastic and glass whose translucency floods the interior with light. Its form is faintly reminiscent of the wooden synagogues of Poland.

Interior of Beth Shalom Synagogue with the Ark at the left. Wright, as was his custom, designed all the interior decoration and furniture, using a sharply geometric style consistent with the architecture.

Main Line Reform Temple (Beth Elohim), Wynne-wood, Pennsylvania. Ehrlich and Levinson, the architects for this contemporary synagogue, have used the circle as the chief design motif, topping the auditorium with a saucer-shaped dome with a skylight. At the left are the bronze doors of the Ark, with sculptured symbolic designs. Slightly left of center is a menorah.

Detail of the Ark in the Wynnewood Synagogue. The doors have been slid open revealing two toroth in velvet covers. The handles of the bronze doors are in the form of the Tablets of the Law — the Ten Commandments — written in Hebrew characters. Over the Ark is the eternal light, one of the features of all synagogues.

Temple Mount Sinai, El Paso, Texas, 1962. The architect, Sidney Eisenshtat, used stone and reinforced concrete in strikingly strong angular forms that seem to reflect the rugged and barren mountains that dominate the landscape.

Christianity

THE CHRISTIAN RELIGION is based on the teachings of Jesus, a Jew who was born in the town of Bethlehem in what is now the country of Israel. At that time the country, like all of the lands surrounding the Mediterranean, had been conquered by the Roman Empire. The Jews of the region, having suffered long under many captivities and dispersions, hoped for and believed in the coming of a Messiah who would reunify and lead them. To many of them Jesus was that person. The Greek word for Messiah is *christos*, from which the name of the religion is derived.

Jesus had a religious experience in which his mission was revealed to him; that mission was to preach the love that God had already revealed. Love was the means by which the kingdom of heaven would be achieved. Love of God and of one's fellow man was the key to salvation, happiness and peace.

So sincere was Jesus when he preached this seemingly simple idea, and so sorely needed was such a philosophy, that his reputation spread. As he traveled from village to village with his message he attracted hundreds of followers, chief among them twelve men called his apostles.

Because of his great popularity and the large number of his followers Jesus was seen as a revolutionary threat both to the Roman occupiers and the established Jewish high priesthood, who depended on the Romans for their power. He was betrayed by Judas, one of his followers, and executed by the Romans. A form of execution at the time was nailing the convicted man to a wooden cross — crucifixion. The cross has ever since been the symbol of Christianity.

On the third day after his burial his tomb was found to be empty by some of his most devout followers, who proclaimed his resurrection. The Resurrection of Jesus — or Christ — is one of the basic beliefs of the Christian religion.

The teachings of Christ were carried on by his followers, two of the most important being Saint Peter and Saint Paul, both of whom traveled widely spreading the new religion to the peoples of Asia, Africa and Europe. Probably the most important factor in the early growth of Christianity was the conversion of the Roman emperor Constantine, who then made Christianity the official religion of the Roman Empire in the fourth century.

In the almost two thousand years that Christianity has existed it has spread to almost every part of the world. But, as with almost all religions, many divisions, groups and sects have developed over the years. The two largest groups are the Roman Catholic and the Eastern Orthodox, and another large group forms the Coptic Church. Among the Protestant groups the largest are the Lutherans, Anglicans, Episcopalians, Presbyterians, Baptists and Methodists.

The scriptures of Christianity are the Old Testament — of Judaism — and the New Testament, which contains the writings of the apostles Matthew, John, Peter and James and their disciples Mark and Luke.

Public worship in Christian churches is congregational in nature. In Roman Catholic, Orthodox, Anglican and Episcopalian churches worship is led by a priest according to a very formal ritual, called a liturgy. The liturgy in Roman Catholic churches, called a mass, includes some congregational participation in oral prayer and song. Protestant worship, led by a minister, traditionally has put more stress on the participation of the worshippers, and on a sermon. Organ music and choir singing are common in many church services.

Christian Churches and Cathedrals

THE EARLIEST CHRISTIAN CHURCHES were built in the form of a basilica, a form borrowed from buildings used by the Romans for business and courts of law. The basilica was a rectangular building with an apse at one end and a central aisle, or nave, flanked by side aisles, and rows of columns separating nave from aisles. The nave tended to be higher than the aisles. The word *church* comes from the Greek word *kuriakon*, meaning the Lord's house.

Eastern Orthodox churches were generally Byzantine in style, built on the plan of a Greek cross with a low dome over the crossing. In Russia, Orthodox churches are topped with one or more domes, usually onion-shaped and sometimes covered with gold leaf. The interiors of both Greek and Russian Orthodox churches are notable for their altar screens covered with richly painted icons.

In western European countries from the tenth through the thirteenth centuries a style called Romanesque was developed, which borrowed from both Roman and Byzantine forms. Usually following the basilica plan, Romanesque churches were characterized by heavy masonry, barrel vaulting over the nave, thick, heavy columns crowned with sculptured capitals, and the use of mosaics or frescoes in the interiors.

During the later Medieval period, generally from the twelfth through the fourteenth centuries, the Gothic style prevailed for churches and cathedrals. Based on the plan of a Latin cross, one of the chief features of Gothic structures was a vertical, soaring quality achieved through the use of slender, ribbed columns that bent inward toward their tops to form pointed arches over the nave. Large stained glass windows, buttresses and lavish sculptural decoration around entrance portals were other characteristics of the Gothic style.

The period of the Renaissance in Europe, roughly from the fourteenth through seventeenth centuries, brought with it a new form of architecture for churches and cathedrals borrowing adaptations of the features of Greek and Roman architecture, such as columns, arches, barrel vaulting and domes. The Baroque style was a development of the late Renaissance in which there was stress on great curving forms and ornateness of details. Architectural forms, sculpture, and painting meld in the interiors to form breathtaking compositions of incredible complexity.

Christian churches in the New World tended to imitate the European forms of church architecture, but with adaptations governed by the materials most readily available in various regions. Since wood is the most abundant material in the Northeast, wooden adaptations of English Renaissance (Georgian) and Greek Revival churches are most prevalent in New England. Brick is the most commonly used material in the Southern states, adobe in the Southwest, and stone and stucco in the Latin American countries.

Contemporary trends in both forms and new materials such as steel and poured concrete are being reflected in church architecture in Europe and the Americas today. Some of the most creative modern architects, departing from tradition, are designing houses of worship in new, exciting and dramatic forms.

Nativity Square in Bethlehem, one of Christendom's holiest shrines. The original basilica was built over the grotto — which is the traditional site of Christ's birth — by the Emperor Constantine. It has been transformed over the years, and because of the need to protect the site has assumed a fortresslike appearance. The main basilica in the background is in the possession of the Greek Orthodox Church, with the Armenian Orthodox using the north apse. The adjoining Church of St. Catherine at the right, founded by the Franciscan order of the Roman Catholic Church, has its own entrance to the Grotto of the Nativity.

Basilica of the Holy Sepulcher, Jerusalem. Chiefly Romanesque in style, this church was built on the reputed site of the tomb of Jesus — and thus is probably the most hallowed church in the Holy Land. It is the common property of three major Christian groups: Roman Catholic, Greek Orthodox and Armenian Orthodox. The building had deteriorated greatly after a long period of neglect. Restoration, necessitating the unsightly scaffolding seen in the picture, has been in process since 1966.

*Interior of the Basilica of the Holy Sepulcher, showing
the altar and apse.*

The Katholikon in Daphni, Greece. Built in the ninth century, it is a typical example of Greek Orthodox churches, which were constructed on the plan of a Greek cross with a dome crowning the crossing of the four arms.

Church of Abba Libanos in Ethiopia. Christianity was adopted as the state religion in the fourth century, and hundreds of Ethiopian Orthodox churches (branches of the Coptic Church) were carved out of solid rock in mountainous country, especially during the Middle Ages.

Church of Saint George, another rock-cut Ethiopian Orthodox Coptic church, rises from a pit. The whole church is cruciform in shape, with three equilateral crosses, one inside the other, as roof decoration.

The Russian Orthodox Church of St. Sophia in Kiev, Soviet Union. Built from 1018 to 1037, this was the first masonry church to be constructed in Russia after the adoption of Christianity there. It has a central dome surrounded by twelve others, symbolizing Christ and the twelve apostles.

Some of the early Russian Orthodox churches were built entirely of wood, as shown in this picture of two log churches on the island of Kizhi in Lake Onega, So-viet Union. The Pokrov Church, octagonal in shape and built in 1764, is in the foreground. Behind it, crowned by 22 onion-shaped domes, is the Preobrazhenye Church built in 1714. The bell tower at the left was added to the complex in 1874.

St. Mark's, Venice, 1042–1058. An example of Byzantine architecture, it has a large central dome, with four smaller domes over each of the arms of the cross which forms its floor plan. Its ornate façade includes five great portals, sculpture, and brilliantly colored mosaics, all created at different periods in its history.

A stave church in Borgund, Norway, built in 1150 soon after the Vikings were Christianized. Constructed of wood, the most plentiful building material in the northern European countries, its steeply pitched roofs easily shed the heavy snow of the region.

Notre-Dame-la-Grande, Poitiers, France. Built in the eleventh and twelfth centuries, this Romanesque church has a façade marked by a profusion of sculptural ornament, much like many of the Indian temples. The heavy stonework and round arches are typical of Romanesque churches.

The Cathedral of Chartres in France, built from 1194 to 1260. One of the most magnificent examples of French Gothic architecture, its spires, soaring over the surrounding wheatfields, can be seen for miles.

Chartres Cathedral dominates the town of Chartres, which grew up around it. The typical cruciform plan, with a nave and transepts, can be seen in this picture, as can the flying buttresses which support the walls.

The façade of Chartres Cathedral, showing its triple portal flanked by sculpture, its stained glass rose window and its dissimilar towers. The tower on the left was not added until 1506 and is in a later, more ornate Gothic style.

Interior of Rheims Cathedral, begun in 1211 and built as a coronation church for the kings of France. The clusters of slender, vertical piers which rise upward forming pointed arches give the interior the soaring character typical of most Gothic cathedrals.

St. Peter's Basilica, Rome, the world's most important Roman Catholic church and one of the finest examples of Renaissance architecture. Built over a period from 1506 to 1626, its final form was a composite of the design of many architects. The original plan was by Bramante, the façade is the work of Maderna, and the dome that of Michelangelo.

Interior of St. Peter's in Rome, showing the main altar, built over the tomb of St. Peter. The canopy, called a baldacchino, was designed by Bernini. There are thirty-three other altars in the huge church.

87

Friends Meeting House, Flushing, New York, 1694, one of the oldest houses of worship in the United States. Completely lacking in ornamentation outside and inside, it is typical of those built by Friends (Quakers), who favor simplicity and plainness in their houses of prayer.

Interior of the Bull's Head Meeting House, Rhinebeck, New York. The extreme plainness reflects the simplicity of the Friends' form of worship, called a meeting.

*Church of San José at the Laguna Pueblo in New
Mexico.* Built 1695–1706 by Franciscan missionaries
from Spain who converted the Indians of the Southwest and West to Christianity. Constructed of adobe,
it is suggestive of a Spanish Renaissance church in its
simplest form. It has been in constant use since its
founding.

Church at Wies in Bavaria, Germany, built 1746–1754.
Designed by Dominikus Zimmermann, the church is
one of the finest examples of the German Baroque
style.

Interior of the Wieskirche, looking toward the main altar. Striking and typical of the Baroque (Rococo) interiors is the way in which architectural features, sculpture and painting flow together, interwoven into a unified composition.

The lush, densely decorated main altar of the Wieskirche, featuring a figure of Christ. Strongly evident is a feeling of activity and movement in the architectural and sculptural features.

Old North Church in Boston, built in 1723, in whose steeple lanterns were hung to warn Paul Revere of the approach of British troops during the American Revolution.

Interior of Old North Church. Box pews such as these are found in many early American Protestant churches. The wealthier families of the congregation had their own boxes, sometimes even furnishing them themselves.

First Baptist Church in Providence, Rhode Island, dedicated in 1775. A fine example of Georgian architecture, this is the house of worship of the oldest Baptist congregation in America, founded by Roger Williams in 1638.

First Congregational Church, Bennington, Vermont, 1806. A carpenter, Lavius Fillmore, based his design for this handsome church on a drawing from Asher Benjamin, who wrote the first original book on architecture to be printed in America. The use of wood, painted white, is typical of hundreds of Protestant churches, especially in New England.

The Mormon Temple in Salt Lake City, Utah. Begun in 1853 on a site designated by the great Mormon leader, Brigham Young, it is built in a unique Victorian style that combines some elements of both Romanesque and Gothic architecture. The figure on the steeple at the right is that of the Angel Moroni. Although it is not a place for public worship, it is used for instruction and sacred ceremonies, including marriages and baptisms.

Grundtvig's Church, Copenhagen, Denmark, 1924–1941. This Lutheran church was named for a well-known nineteenth-century clergyman who founded the folk school movement. Built of polished yellow bricks, it was designed by Peter Vilhelm Klint, who was one of the first architects in Europe to depart from traditional church architecture.

*Chapel of Notre-Dame-du-Haut at Ronchamp, France,
1950–1954.* In this small Roman Catholic church of
poured concrete, Le Corbusier, Swiss-born architect,
has invented a bold and daring form, departing from
any traditional concept of church architecture. At the
right is an outdoor altar and pulpit.

Interior of Le Corbusier's chapel at Ronchamp. The nichelike window treatment was inspired by niches of a mosque in El Aleut in Algeria that were cut into the thick walls to hold the worshippers' shoes.

Wayfarers' Chapel at Portuguese Bend, California. A Swedenborgian church, this striking structure of glass and redwood was designed by Lloyd Wright. On a high bluff overlooking the Pacific, it affords worshippers a view of the ocean.

Church of Notre Dame at Royan, France. Designed by Guillaume Gillet and built in 1958, after the town of Royan had been almost completely destroyed by bombs during World War II. It is of reinforced concrete, rising boldly and starkly above the low buildings of the town.

Cathedral of St. Michael, Coventry, England. The fifteenth-century Gothic cathedral was almost totally destroyed during the bombing of Coventry in World War II (1940). Instead of rebuilding it in its former style the architect, Sir Basil Spence, felt that its reconstruction should be in a spirit as relevant to today as the medieval builder was to his day. The new building, consecrated in 1962, of steel, glass and reinforced concrete, rises amid the ruins of the old church as a striking contrast.

Another view of St. Michael's Cathedral in Coventry.
The bronze figures of St. Michael vanquishing the
demon are by the sculptor Sir Jacob Epstein.

St. Mary's Cathedral, San Francisco, 1965–1971. Designed by McSweeney, Ryan and Lee, with Pietro Bel-
luschi and the Italian architect Luigi Nervi as consul-
tants, this contemporary Roman Catholic cathedral is
the first in which more space is set aside for community
and social use than for worship.

*The interior of St. Mary's Cathedral, showing the bal-
dacchino, a sculpture of aluminum rods by Richard
Lippold, suspended by wires 75 feet above the altar.*

A drive-in church in Sarasota, Florida. A product of the automobile age, such churches have become popular in the United States since the 1950's. Loudspeakers are available for each car as in drive-in theaters.

An Easter sunrise service at Mirror Lake in Yosemite National Park, California. Worship in outdoor settings of special natural beauty has become popular among many Protestant groups in the United States.

Revival meeting under the canvas of a huge tent. Since
the middle of the nineteenth century such services con-
ducted by itinerant Protestant ministers who carry their
own "house of worship" with them have been popular
in the United States.

A storefront church in New York. Such churches, a new phenomenon, are springing up in great numbers, usually in economically disadvantaged urban areas.

Islam

ISLAM — the word comes from the Arabic meaning submission to the will of God — was founded in the seventh century by a man later known as the prophet Mohammed. Born in Mecca in what is now Saudi Arabia, Mohammed, although illiterate, was a thinker and he found distasteful the idol worship of the desert Arabs of the region.

Mecca at that time was an important trading center to which caravans came from all over the Middle East. It was also a pilgrimage site for worshippers from all over Arabia who came annually to pray at a shrine called the Kaaba, which was comprised of several hundred idols and a black meteorite.

From his contact with the Jews and Christians of the caravans Mohammed gained knowledge of their religions and acquired a profound respect for them, with their stress on the worship of one God.

Not unlike Abraham and Buddha before him, he had what might be called a revelation through a vision. Although apprehensive at first about the vision he was eventually convinced of its validity and of the idea that he had been chosen as the prophet of the one and only true God, Allah. His revelations were eventually compiled in a sacred book, the Koran, the scriptures of Islam.

Mohammed, in speaking out publicly against idol worship, was a threat to the merchant families of Mecca who thrived on the business brought to their city by pilgrims. He was finally forced to flee for his life to the friendlier city of Yathrib, later called Medina. The flight, termed the Hegira, was made in 622, the year from which Moslem calendars are dated.

In Medina Mohammed became an influential religious and political leader. Having gained a considerable following he reentered Mecca, smashed the idols, and proclaimed the Black Stone of the Kaaba the holiest site of Islam.

Islam quickly gained thousands of converts — called Mohammedans, or more commonly Moslems. After Mohammed's death Islam spread rapidly eastward as far as India and westward across North Africa — as far as Spain and France.

A Moslem believes that there is only one God, Allah, and that he has revealed himself through the prophets — including all the Hebrew prophets and Jesus — and that Mohammed was the last of them, or the "Seal of the Prophets." Although Mohammed did not provide for an organized priesthood or sacraments, he prescribed many observances, the five key ones called the Five Pillars of Islam.

According to the Five Pillars of Islam, Moslems are required to:

- Recite the creed.
- Pray five times daily.
- Fast during the holy month of Ramadan.
- Give alms to the poor.
- Make a pilgrimage to Mecca once during a lifetime.

Group worship is practiced by Moslems. Worshippers congregate at specific times, bowing and kneeling at certain intervals. Prayer, which includes readings from the Koran, is led by a pious member of the congregation.

Mosques

MOSQUES, the buildings erected by Moslems as their places of worship, differ in style from one part of the Moslem world to another, and also according to when they were built. Some mosques, especially in the larger Moslem capitals like Damascus, Cairo, Jerusalem and Istanbul, are extremely huge and complex structures, while village mosques may be very small and simple.

Common to all mosques, however, small or large, simple or grand, are five chief features:

• The mihrab, which is a niche in the inside of the wall that faces Mecca — called the qibla wall — and toward which the worshipper faces while praying.

• The minbar, a raised pulpit, usually with a staircase leading to it, and often with a canopy over it.

• A screen, sometimes forming an enclosure around the mihrab.

• A desk, or stand, on which the Koran rests.

• A fountain or pool for the ablutions of the worshipper. Islamic law decrees that worshippers shall wash hands and feet and various other parts of the body before praying.

One or more minarets are almost always a feature of a mosque. A minaret is the tower from which the muezzin calls the faithful to prayer five times a day. The muezzin, however, has largely been replaced in this electronic age by a recording emanating from a loudspeaker atop the minaret.

The interiors of most mosques are notable for their large, uncluttered open floor spaces, usually covered with Oriental rugs on which worshippers sit or kneel in prayer. Mosques are marked by their absence of any images of man or animal since Islamic law forbids the representation of such figures. Instead, many mosques boast very rich ornament of geometric designs and Arabic inscriptions from the Koran executed in colored tile, mosaic, or carved in plaster. Such ornamentation can be found on both the interior and exterior of mosques.

The Great Mosque in Mecca, the spiritual center of the Moslem world. The plain, black cubic building in the mosque's courtyard houses the Kaaba, the stone declared by Mohammed to be Islam's holiest site.

The Dome of the Rock, Jerusalem, seventh century.
Built by the Caliph Abd al-Malik, it stands in a large
enclosure formerly the site of the original Jewish
Temple. The golden dome is set over an octagonal ro-
tunda covered with designs in colored marble and tiles.
Directly under the dome is a huge exposed rock which
is the legendary site of Abraham's sacrifice and also of
Mohammed's ascent to heaven.

*Interior of the Dome of the Rock, showing a section of
the ambulatory or rotunda that surrounds the rock.*
The earliest existing monument of Moslem architecture,
it is remarkable for the richness of its mosaic, marble
and gold ornament.

Great Mosque of Qairawan, Tunisia, begun in 670. The earliest of all North African mosques, its form is typical of much oasis architecture. Centered around an arcaded courtyard, it presents a blank, sometimes fortified wall to the outside.

Courtyard of the Mosque of Ahmad ibn Tulun in Cairo, Egypt, 876–879. The domed well in the center of its courtyard shows its derivation from oasis architecture. The minaret was developed from the watchtower and is a landmark for travelers.

Exterior of the great mosque at Cordova, Spain. The
Emperor Charles V had the mosque transformed into a
Christian church in the sixteenth century.

Interior of the mosque at Cordova, begun in 786. This magnificent monument to the Arab conquest of Spain features a forest of double-tiered arches banded in brick and stone.

A dome of the Al Azhar Mosque in Cairo, 970–972.
The mosque is part of the university of the same name,
founded a thousand years ago and still one of the foremost centers of Islamic learning.

Al Azhar Mosque. This photograph shows part of the arcade that surrounds three sides of the courtyard.

Entrance gateway to the Masjid-i-Jami (the Friday Mosque) in Isfahan, Iran. Originally built in the tenth century, it was enlarged and remodeled through the seventeenth century. In the courtyard is a pool used for the ritual ablutions required by Islamic law. The elaborate tile ornament covering the surface is typical of Persian Islamic architecture.

The mihrab in the Masjid-i-Jami in Isfahan, flanked on each side by a minbar.

Detail of the entrance to Masjid-i-Shah, or Shah Mosque, in Isfahan, Iran. The stalactite formation is typical of Moslem architecture of Iran, Morocco and Spain. The glazed tiles combine floral and geometric patterns and Arabic script in flowing tapestrylike designs that cover the whole surface.

The Mosque of Sheikh Lotfollah in Isfahan, built by order of the great Shah Abbas I in the seventeenth century for his personal use. The dome is covered with glazed tiles of various colors on a soft yellow background. The tiles surrounding the entrance are blue.

Selimiye Mosque in Edirne, Turkey, 1568–1575. Designed by the architect Sinan, who considered this his
masterpiece, it is based on an octagonal plan topped by
one of the world's largest domes. Four very slender,
pointed minarets rise from the four corners.

*Interior of the Suleymaniyeh Mosque in Istanbul, six-
teenth century.* The chief mosque of the city, it was the
work of Sinan and is similar in form to his Selimiye
Mosque in Edirne. The vast interior is lighted by hundreds of oil lamps and its floor is covered by prayer
rugs.

Mosque in Marrakech, Morocco. Of reddish brick, the shape of the squat, square minaret is typical of those of the North African countries.

Jami Masjid Mosque, Old Delhi, India, 1650–1656. It was built by Shah Jahan, the emperor who was responsible for the construction of the Taj Mahal. A strikingly magnificent building with three great white marble domes striped with black. The forms of its minarets and onion domes are typical of Indian mosques.

Tuareg Mosque in the Tassili Mountains of Algeria.
The Tuareg people are one of the nomadic Berber
tribes of North Africa. Although fiercely independent,
they adopted Islam. These stones are not a ruin; they
constitute a crude mosque for the desert nomads.

Modern mosque in Mopti, a town in Mali, one of the newer African states. Built of sun-dried clay (similar to the adobe used in the southwestern United States), with wood supports jutting out, it has a sculpturesque quality and is typical of the desert architecture of the region.

Prayer five times daily is required of every faithful Moslem. Here, two Arabs have stopped on a journey in the desert to kneel in prayer, facing Mecca.

Glossary

ADOBE. Sun-dried clay used as a building material.

ALMEMOR. Reader's platform. Term used in German synagogues.

ANTARALA. Vestibule in front of the cella in Hindu temples.

APSE. A semicircular recess at the end of a nave.

ARCH. A curving structure made of wedge-shaped stones or bricks, spanning an opening and capable of supporting a wall above it.

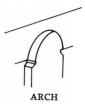

ARCH

ARK. Cupboard or covered niche in a synagogue, in which is kept the Torah.

ASHKENAZIC. Pertaining to the Jews of central and Eastern Europe or their descendants.

BALDACCHINO. A canopy used over the altar, especially in Renaissance and Baroque churches.

BALUSTRADE. A handrail, usually supported by small pillars (balusters).

BALUSTRADE

BAROQUE. The style of the late Renaissance (seventeenth and early eighteenth centuries); usually extremely ornate.

BASILICA. Form of early Christian churches based on plan of Roman public buildings primarily used as law courts.

BIMAH. Reader's platform. Term used in Eastern European synagogues.

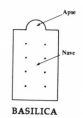

BASILICA

BODHISATTVA. A Buddhist who has attained enlightenment but who has postponed Nirvana in order to help others attain enlightenment. Worshipped as a deity in Mahayana Buddhism.

BOT. Main chapel of Buddhist temple in Southeast Asian countries.

BUTTRESS. Exterior wall support or brace used chiefly in Gothic cathedrals.

BUTTRESS

BYZANTINE. Architectural style of the Byzantine Empire (founded by Constantine in the fifth century with Constantinople as its capital). Chief characteristics of Byzantine churches were the Greek cross floor plan, low domes on a square base, round arches, capitals with foliage patterns, and much use of mosaics and frescoes.

CAPITAL. Top or crown of a column, larger in diameter than the shaft, and usually decorated.

CAPITAL

CATHEDRAL. The principal church of a diocese, containing the bishop's throne.

CELLA. Small chamber of an Indian temple in which is housed the object of worship.

COLONNADE

COLUMN

CORNICE

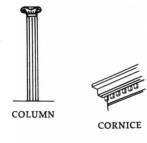

CRUCIFORM

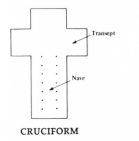

FLYING BUTTRESS

GABLE

GREEK CROSS

LATIN CROSS

CHATTRI. A pointed, umbrella-shaped dome in Indian architecture.

CHEDI. A bell-shaped structure usually related to stupas and pagodas of Southeast Asia.

CHIGI. The continuation of crossed gable-end boards which form a v-shaped projection above the ridge of a Shinto shrine.

COLONNADE. Rows of columns connected at their top by a cornice, and sometimes roofed.

COLUMN. Vertical shaft, cylindrical in form, usually used to support some part of a building.

CORNICE. A horizontal projection at the top of a wall; often a decorative development of the eaves of a roof.

CRUCIFORM. With a cross-shaped floor plan.

DIASPORA. The scattering of the Jews to countries outside of Palestine following the Babylonian conquest.

FAÇADE. The front or chief elevation of a building, usually containing the main entrance.

FLYING BUTTRESS. An openwork masonry support used to resist the outward thrust of the wall of a Gothic church or cathedral.

GABLE. The triangular portion of the end wall of a building.

GABLE ROOF. Roof with two sloping sides and triangular gables at both ends.

GARBHA-GRIHA. Womb-cell or holiest part of an Indian temple.

GEORGIAN. Architectural style in England based on that of the Italian Renaissance. Named for the first four King Georges (1714–1830).

GOPURAM. In Indian architecture, the large gate tower of a temple enclosure.

GOTHIC. Late Medieval style in Europe (thirteenth and fourteenth centuries) characterized by pointed arches, buttresses, stone tracery, stained glass windows.

GREEK CROSS. A cross with four equal arms.

ICON. An image or painting, usually of a sacred person.

IMAM. Moslem religious leader of the community.

KAMI. The Shinto gods of Japan.

KIBLA. The wall or part of a mosque on the side nearest Mecca.

KIOSK. A light, open pavilion or summerhouse often supported by pillars.

LATIN CROSS. A cross with one arm longer than the other three.

MAIDAN. Square or plaza in India or Iran.

MANDAPA. Large open hall of an Indian temple.

MASONRY. Construction using stone or brick, with mortar.

MENORAH. Seven-branched candelabrum used in the original Temple in Jerusalem. A nine-branched version is used in the celebration of the Jewish festival of Chanukah.

MIHRAB. A niche in the kibla wall or any other part of a mosque facing Mecca.

MINARET. A tall, usually slender tower, connected with a mosque, from which the muezzin calls the faithful to prayer.

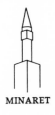

MINARET

MINBAR. The pulpit of a mosque, usually at the top of a short flight of steps.

MONOTHEISM. The belief that there is only one God.

MOSAIC. Small cubes of glass or stone set in cement to form designs or pictures.

MUEZZIN. A crier who calls Moslems to prayer five times daily from a minaret.

NAVE. The central space of a basilica, church, or cathedral, usually running the greater part of the length of the building.

PANTHEON. All the gods of a religion.

PATRIARCH. The father or head of a family or tribe.

PIER. Masonry support for an arch.

PIER

PILASTER. A flattened column usually used decoratively.

PRANG. A structure in Southeast Asia shaped like a corncob.

PUEBLO. Spanish word for town, used for the multiple dwellings of some of the Southwest Indians.

PILASTER

RENAISSANCE. The period in Europe (roughly the fourteenth through the seventeenth centuries) which saw the rebirth of classical (Greek and Roman) art forms.

RIWAQ. An arcade surrounding the central courtyard of a mosque.

ROCOCO. Highly ornate style of the late Baroque period.

ROMANESQUE. Architectural style (roughly tenth through twelfth centuries) characterized by heavy masonry, round arches, and barrel vaulting.

SEPHARDIC. Pertaining to the Jews of Spain and Portugal or their descendants.

SIKHARA. Tower or spire over the sanctuary of an Indian temple.

STALACTITE. Ceiling ornament in Islamic architecture.

STUPA. Originally a Buddhist burial mound; later a cylindrical or dome-shaped building housing relics of Buddha or his apostles.

TEBAH. Reader's platform. Term used in Sephardic synagogues.

TORAH. The first five books of the Old Testament (the Pentateuch) traditionally handwritten on a scroll of parchment (sheep- or goatskin).

TORII. Gate or entrance to a Shinto shrine.

TOROTH. Hebrew plural of Torah.

TRANSEPT. The part of a cruciform church at right angles to the nave.

TRIMURTI. Word for the Hindu Trinity.

VAULT. An arched ceiling or roof, usually of stone or brick.

VAULT

VIHARN. Repository for sacred objects in Buddhist temples of Southeast Asia.

VIMANA. Towered sanctuary of Indian temples.

WAT. Word for Buddhist temple complex in Southeast Asian countries.

Bibliography

REFERENCES ON RELIGIONS

Forman, Henry James, and Roland Gammon, *Truth Is One*. New York: Harper, 1954. Good text on ten chief living religions, with hundreds of black and white photographs.

Great Religions of the World. Washington: National Geographic Society, 1971. Text by scholars in each religion. Excerpts from the scriptures of each religion. Beautifully and lavishly illustrated in color.

Zaehner, R. C. (ed.), *The Concise Encyclopedia of Living Faiths*. New York: Hawthorn Books, 1959. Excellent text, with sections on each religion written by different experts.

REFERENCES ON ARCHITECTURE — GENERAL SURVEYS

Anson, Peter F., *The Building of Churches*. London: Burns & Oates, 1962 (vol. 10 in The New Library of Catholic Knowledge). Excellent, concise history of Christian places of worship. Lavishly illustrated in black and white and color.

Collier's Encyclopedia. Good section on architecture, including many black and white photographs and well-illustrated glossary of architectural terms.

Copplestone, Trewin (ed.), *World Architecture*. London: Hamlyn, 1963. A large, handsome book with hundreds of photographs in black and white, some full-page color photographs, drawings, and text.

Fletcher, Banister, *A History of Architecture on the Comparative Method*. New York: Scribner's, 1961. Large, exhaustive work, illustrated with hundreds of black and white photographs, drawings of details and floor plans.

Gardner, Helen, *Art Through the Ages* (revised by Horst de la Croix and Richard G. Tansey). New York: Harcourt, Brace & World, 1970. Excellent general survey of western art and architecture. Clearly written and lavishly illustrated sections on architecture, especially Romanesque, Gothic and Renaissance.

Hamlin, Talbot F., *Architecture Through the Ages*. New York: Putnam, 1940. Excellent interpretation of architecture in civilization. Mostly text.

SEWALL, JOHN IVES, *A History of Western Art*. New York: Holt, Rinehart, and Winston, 1961. Very explicit and well-illustrated sections on structural principles of the arch, vault, dome, Early Christian, Romanesque and Gothic architecture.

UPJOHN, E. M., P. S. WINGERT, and J. G. MAHLER, *History of World Art*. New York: Oxford University Press, 1958. Good, well-illustrated general survey. Includes western and eastern architecture.

REFERENCES ON ARCHITECTURE — SPECIFIC PERIODS AND COUNTRIES

ALEX, WILLIAM, *Japanese Architecture*. New York: George Braziller, 1963. Concise text. Excellent black and white photographs, drawings and floor plans.

AUBOYER, JEANNINE, and ROGER GOEPPER, *The Oriental World*. New York: McGraw-Hill, 1967. A volume in the series Landmarks of the World's Art. Text, beautifully illustrated in black and white and color.

BRODERICK, ROBERT C., *Historic Churches of the United States*. New York: Wilfred Funk, 1958. Good historical survey of houses of worship in the United States, well illustrated with black and white photographs. Includes mostly churches, but a few non-Christian examples.

GIESELMANN, REINHARD, *New Churches*. New York: Architectural Book Publishing Co., 1972. Striking black and white photographs with some text on the latest church architecture of Europe and the United States.

GOVERNMENT OF INDIA, DEPARTMENT OF TOURISM, *The Temples of India*. Delhi: 1964 (abridged edition, 1968). Hindu and Buddhist temples of all periods and regions of India. Lavishly illustrated in black and white.

GRUBE, ERNEST J., *The World of Islam*. New York: McGraw-Hill, 1966. A volume in the series Landmarks of the World's Art. Text, beautifully illustrated in black and white and color.

HOAG, JOHN D., *Western Islamic Architecture*. New York: George Braziller, 1963. Concise text. Excellent black and white photographs, drawings and floor plans.

KAMPF, AVRAM, *Contemporary Synagogue Art*. New York: Union of American Hebrew Congregations, 1966. Brief historical background. Text and good photographs of synagogues and their decorative details.

Lassus, Jean, *The Early Christian and Byzantine World*. New York: McGraw-Hill, 1967. A volume in the series Landmarks of the World's Art. Text, beautifully illustrated in black and white and color.

Millon, Henry. *Baroque and Rococo Architecture*. New York: George Braziller, 1961. Concise text. Excellent black and white photographs, drawings and floor plans.

Smith, G. E. Kidder, *The New Churches of Europe*. New York: Holt, Rinehart, and Winston, 1964. Excellent photographs, including details and floor plans, with short text on each church.

Wischnitzer, Rachel, *Synagogue Architecture in the United States*. Philadelphia: The Jewish Publication Society of America, 1955. Text, illustrated with photographs, engravings, drawings, floor plans.

———— *The Architecture of the European Synagogue*. Philadelphia: The Jewish Publication Society of America, 1964. Comprehensive text, illustrated with photographs, engravings, drawings, floor plans.

Wu, Nelson I., *Chinese and Indian Architecture*. New York: George Braziller, 1963. Concise text. Excellent black and white photographs, drawings and floor plans.

BOOKS WRITTEN SPECIFICALLY FOR YOUNG PEOPLE

Fitch, Florence Mary, *One God: The Ways We Worship Him*. New York: Lothrop, Lee & Shepard, 1944. Excellent text on Judaism, Christianity and Islam, with several photographs.

———— *Their Search for God: Ways of Worship in the Orient*. New York: Lothrop, Lee & Shepard, 1947. Fine text on Hinduism, Buddhism, the Chinese philosophies and Shinto, with several photographs.

Life, the Editorial Staff of, *The World's Great Religions*. New York: Golden Press, 1958. Young people's edition of the original *Life* publication. Text and color illustrations on Hinduism, Buddhism, the Chinese philosophies, Shinto, Judaism, Christianity, Islam.

Savage, Katherine, *The Story of World Religions*. New York: Henry Z. Walck, 1967. Very good text, illustrated with maps and photographs.

Sources of Illustrations

(The numbers given are page numbers.)

Air India   10, 21 top

Wayne Andrews   58, 61, 63, 91 top, 98, 100

Donald Becker   9 top, 28, 33, 43, 57, 121, 122 top, 127

The Bettmann Archive   16, 26, 114, 124, 125, 128

British Tourist Authority   102, 103

Chen-Woo Wu   30

Egyptian Tourist Office   115, 118, 119

French Government Tourist Office   81, 82, 83, 84, 85, 99, 101

German National Tourist Office   90, 91 bottom

Government of India Tourist Office   13 top

Government of India Tourist Office, Chicago   8, 9 bottom, 12 top, 14, 15

Government of India Tourist Office, New York   20

Government of India Tourist Office, San Francisco   21 bottom, 22

Greek National Tourist Office   Frontispiece

Carl E. Hiller   79, 86, 95

Information Service of India   6, 11

Iran Air   122 bottom

Iran National Tourist Office   120

Israel Government Tourist Office   49, 50, 71, 72, 73, 113 top

Japan National Tourist Office   24

Japan National Tourist Organization   25, 37, 38, 39, 40, 41, 42, 44

Jewish Theological Seminary   59

Nathaniel Lieberman   88 bottom, 108

Marburg–Art Reference Bureau   74, 77, 113 bottom

Netherlands National Travel Office   56

Pacific Area Travel Association   12 bottom, 13 bottom, 27, 29

Photo-Kulturinstitut, Worms. Photo supplied by the Leo Baeck Institute   51 top

Religious News Service   80, 87, 88 top, 89, 93, 94, 96, 97, 105, 106, 107

Society of Friends of Touro Synagogue National Historic Shrine   58 top

Sovphoto   71

Spanish National Tourist Office   53, 116, 117

Spanish National Tourist Office, Chicago   52

Tadesse Araya   75, 76

Tourist Organization of Thailand   23, 31, 32, 34

Turkish Government Tourism and Information Office   123

Union of American Hebrew Congregations/Charles Kanarian   60

Union of American Hebrew Congregations/Jules Schick   65

Union of American Hebrew Congregations/Julius Shulman   66

Union of American Hebrew Congregations/Jacob Stelman   64

Wide World Photos   92, 112

Gene Wright   104

YIVO Institute for Jewish Research   51 bottom, 54, 55

Index

Ohio Dominican College
J 726 H, RARE, BOOK, ROOM
Hiller, Carl E.
Caves to cathedrals

3 5270 00032019 0

DATE DUE

DOES NOT CIRCULATE

J 726 H RARE BOOK ROOM
Hiller, Carl E.
Caves to cathedrals

Ohio Dominican College Library
1216 Sunbury Road
Columbus, Ohio 43219

GAYLORD M2G